Mean Time

Best wishes

ALSO BY CAROL ANN DUFFY

CAROL ANN DUFFY

Mean Time

ANVIL PRESS POETRY

Published in 1993
by Anvil Press Poetry Ltd
69 King George Street London SE10 8PX
Reprinted in 1993

This book is published
with financial assistance from
The Arts Council

Designed and composed by Anvil
Photoset in Plantin by Wordstream
Printed and bound in England
by Morganprint Blackheath Ltd

ISBN 0 85646 247 0

A catalogue record for this book
is available from the British Library

ACKNOWLEDGEMENTS

Some of these poems have appeared in the following: *The
American Scholar*, *Aquarius*, BBC Radio, *The Independent on
Sunday*, *New Statesman*, *New Writing* (Minerva/British
Council), The Oscars Press, *Poetry Book Society Anthology
1991*, *Poetry Review*, Bernard Stone/Turret Books, *The
Sunday Times*, *The Times*, *The Times Literary Supplement*,
Verse.

Thanks are due for an Arts Council Writers' Bursary in 1992.

CONTENTS

THE CAPTAIN OF THE 1964
TOP OF THE FORM TEAM

Do Wah Diddy Diddy, *Baby Love*, *Oh Pretty Woman*
were in the Top Ten that month, October, and the Beatles
were everywhere else. I can give you the B-side
of the Supremes one. Hang on. *Come See About Me?*
I lived in a kind of fizzing hope. Gargling
with Vimto. The clever smell of my satchel. Convent girls.
I pulled my hair forward with a steel comb that I blew
like Mick, my lips numb as a two-hour snog.

No snags. The Nile rises in April. Blue and White.
The humming-bird's song is made by its wings, which beat
so fast that they blur in flight. I knew the capitals,
the Kings and Queens, the dates. In class, the white sleeve
of my shirt saluted again and again. *Sir!* . . . *Correct.*
Later, I whooped at the side of my bike, a cowboy,
mounted it running in one jump. I sped down Dyke Hill,
no hands, famous, learning, *dominus domine dominum.*

Dave Dee Dozy . . . Try me. Come on. My mother kept my
      mascot Gonk
on the TV set for a year. And the photograph. I look
so brainy you'd think I'd just had a bath. The blazer.
The badge. The tie. The first chord of *A Hard Day's Night*
loud in my head. I ran to the Spinney in my prize shoes,
up Churchill Way, up Nelson Drive, over pink pavements
that girls chalked on, in a blue evening; and I stamped
the pawprints of badgers and skunks in the mud. My
      country.

I want it back. The captain. The one with all the answers.
      Bzz.
My name was in red on Lucille Green's jotter. I smiled

as wide as a child who went missing on the way home
from school. The keeny. I say to my stale wife
Six hits by Dusty Springfield. I say to my boss *A pint!*
How can we know the dancer from the dance? Nobody.
My thick kids wince. *Name the Prime Minister of Rhodesia.*
My country. *How many florins in a pound?*

LITANY

The soundtrack then was a litany – *candlewick*
bedspread three piece suite display cabinet –
and stiff-haired wives balanced their red smiles,
passing the catalogue. *Pyrex.* A tiny ladder
ran up Mrs Barr's American Tan leg, sly
like a rumour. Language embarrassed them.

The terrible marriages crackled, cellophane
round polyester shirts, and then The Lounge
would seem to bristle with eyes, hard
as the bright stones in engagement rings,
and sharp hands poised over biscuits as a word
was spelled out. An embarrassing word, broken

to bits, which tensed the air like an accident.
This was the code I learnt at my mother's knee, pretending
to read, where no one had cancer, or sex, or debts,
and certainly not leukaemia, which no one could spell.
The year a mass grave of wasps bobbed in a jam-jar;
a butterfly stammered itself in my curious hands.

A boy in the playground, I said, *told me*
to fuck off; and a thrilled, malicious pause
salted my tongue like an imminent storm. Then
uproar. *I'm sorry, Mrs Barr, Mrs Hunt, Mrs Emery,*
sorry, Mrs Raine. Yes, I can summon their names.
My mother's mute shame. The taste of soap.

NOSTALGIA

Those early mercenaries, it made them ill –
leaving the mountains, leaving the high, fine air
to go down, down. What they got
was money, dull crude coins clenched
in the teeth; strange food, the wrong taste,
stones in the belly; and the wrong sounds,
the wrong smells, the wrong light, every breath –
wrong. They had an ache *here*, Doctor,
they pined, wept, grown men. It was killing them.

It was given a name. Hearing tell of it,
there were those who stayed put, fearful
of a sweet pain in the heart; of how it hurt,
in that heavier air, to hear
the music of home – the sad pipes – summoning,
in the dwindling light of the plains,
a particular place – where maybe you met a girl,
or searched for a yellow ball in long grass,
found it just as your mother called you in.

But the word was out. Some would never
fall in love had they not heard of love.
So the priest stood at the stile with his head
in his hands, crying at the workings of memory
through the colour of leaves, and the schoolteacher
opened a book to the scent of her youth, too late.
It was spring when one returned, with his life
in a sack on his back, to find the same street
with the same sign on the inn, the same bell
chiming the hour on the clock, and everything changed.

STAFFORD AFTERNOONS

Only there, the afternoons could suddenly pause
and when I looked up from lacing my shoe
a long road held no one, the gardens were empty,
an ice-cream van chimed and dwindled away.

On the motorway bridge, I waved at windscreens,
oddly hurt by the blurred waves back, the speed.
So I let a horse in the noisy field sponge at my palm
and invented, in colour, a vivid lie for us both.

In a cul-de-sac, a strange boy threw a stone.
I crawled through a hedge into long grass
at the edge of a small wood, lonely and thrilled.
The green silence gulped once and swallowed me whole.

I knew it was dangerous. The way the trees
drew sly faces from light and shade, the wood
let out its sticky breath on the back of my neck,
and flowering nettles gathered spit in their throats.

Too late. *Touch*, said the long-haired man
who stood, legs apart, by a silver birch
with a living, purple root in his hand. The sight
made sound rush back; birds, a distant lawnmower,

his hoarse, frightful endearments as I backed away
then ran all the way home; into a game
where children scattered and shrieked
and time fell from the sky like a red ball.

BROTHERS

Once, I slept in a bed with these four men who share
an older face and can be made to laugh, even now,
at random quotes from the play we were in. *There's no way
in the creation of God's earth*, I say. They grin and nod.

What was possible retreats and shrinks, and in my other eyes
they shrink to an altar boy, a boy practising scales,
a boy playing tennis with a wall, a baby
crying in the night like a new sound flailing for a shape.

Occasionally, when people ask, I enjoy reciting their names.
I don't have photographs, but I like to repeat the names.
My mother chose them. I hear her life in the words,
the breeding words, the word that broke her heart.

Much in common, me, with thieves and businessmen,
fathers and UB40s. We have nothing to say of now,
but time owns us. How tall they have grown. One day
I shall pay for a box and watch them shoulder it.

BEFORE YOU WERE MINE

I'm ten years away from the corner you laugh on
with your pals, Maggie McGeeney and Jean Duff.
The three of you bend from the waist, holding
each other, or your knees, and shriek at the pavement.
Your polka-dot dress blows round your legs. Marilyn.

I'm not here yet. The thought of me doesn't occur
in the ballroom with the thousand eyes, the fizzy, movie
    tomorrows
the right walk home could bring. I knew you would dance
like that. Before you were mine, your Ma stands at the close
with a hiding for the late one. You reckon it's worth it.

The decade ahead of my loud, possessive yell was the best
    one, eh?
I remember my hands in those high-heeled red shoes, relics,
and now your ghost clatters toward me over George Square
till I see you, clear as scent, under the tree,
with its lights, and whose small bites on your neck,
    sweetheart?

Cha cha cha! You'd teach me the steps on the way home from
    Mass,
stamping stars from the wrong pavement. Even then
I wanted the bold girl winking in Portobello, somewhere
in Scotland, before I was born. That glamorous love lasts
where you sparkle and waltz and laugh before you were
    mine.

WELLTREAD

Welltread was Head and the Head's face was a fist. Yes,
I've got him. Spelling and Punishment. A big brass bell
dumb on his desk till only he shook it, and children
ran shrieking in the locked yard. Mr Welltread. Sir.

He meant well. They all did then. The loud, inarticulate
    dads,
the mothers who spat on hankies and rubbed you away.
But Welltread looked like a gangster. Welltread stalked
the forms, collecting thruppenny bits in a soft black hat.

We prayed for Aberfan, vaguely reprieved. My socks
    dissolved,
two grey pools at my ankles, at the shock of my name
called out. The memory brings me to my feet
as a foul would. The wrong child for a trite crime.

And all I could say was *No*. Welltread straightened my hand
as though he could read the future there, then hurt himself
more than he hurt me. There was no cause for complaint.
There was the burn of a cane in my palm, still smouldering.

CONFESSION

Come away into this dark cell and tell
your sins to a hidden man your guardian angel
works your conscience like a glove-puppet It
smells in here doesn't it does it smell
like a coffin how would you know C'mon
out with them sins those little maggoty things
that wriggle in the soul . . . *Bless me Father* . . .

Just how bad have you been there's no water
in hell merely to think of a wrong's as evil
as doing it . . . *For I have sinned* . . . Penance
will cleanse you like a bar of good soap so
say the words into the musty gloom aye
on your knees let's hear that wee voice
recite transgression in the manner approved . . . *Forgive me* . . .

You do well to stammer A proper respect
for eternal damnation see the flicker
of your white hands clasping each other like
Hansel and Gretel in the big black wood
cross yourself Remember the vinegar and sponge
there's light on the other side of the door . . . *Mother
of God* . . . if you can only reach it Jesus loves you.

THE GOOD TEACHERS

You run round the back to be in it again.
No bigger than your thumbs, those virtuous women
size you up from the front row. Soon now,
Miss Ross will take you for double History.
You breathe on the glass, making a ghost of her, say
South Sea Bubble Defenestration of Prague.

You love Miss Pirie. So much, you are top
of her class. So much, you need two of you
to stare out from the year, serious, passionate.
The River's Tale by Rudyard Kipling by heart.
Her kind intelligent green eye. Her cruel blue one.
You are making a poem up for her in your head.

But not Miss Sheridan. Comment vous appelez.
But not Miss Appleby. Equal to the square
of the other two sides. Never Miss Webb.
Dar es Salaam. Kilimanjaro. Look. The good teachers
swish down the corridor in long, brown skirts,
snobbish and proud and clean and qualified.

And they've got your number. You roll the waistband
of your skirt over and over, all leg, all
dumb insolence, smoke-rings. You won't pass.
You could do better. But there's the wall you climb
into dancing, lovebites, marriage, the Cheltenham
and Gloucester, today. The day you'll be sorry one day.

LIKE EARNING A LIVING

What's an elephant like? I say
to the slack-mouthed girl
who answers back, a trainee ventriloquist,
then smirks at Donna. She dunno.
Nor does the youth with the face.
And what would that say, fingered?
I know. Video. Big Mac. Lager. Lager.
What like's a wart-hog? Come on.

Ambition. Rage. Boredom. Spite. How
do they taste, smell, sound?
Nobody cares. Jason doesn't. Nor does his dad.
He met a poet. Didn't know it. Uungh.
What would that aftershave say
if it could think? What colour's the future?

Somewhere in England, Major-Balls,
the long afternoon empties of air, meaning, energy, point.
Kin-L. There just aren't the words for it.
Darren. Paul. Kelly. Marie. What's it like? Mike?

Like earning a living.
Earning a living like.

THE CLICHÉ KID

I need help, Doc, and bad; I can't forget
the rustle of my father's ballgown as he bent
to say goodnight to me, his kiss, his French scent . . .

Give me a shot of something. Or the sound of Ma
and her pals up late, boozing, dealing the cards.
Big Bertha pissing out from the porch under the stars . . .

It gets worse. Chalkdust. The old schoolroom empty.
This kid so unpopular even my imaginary friend left me
for another child. I'm screwed up, Doc, jumpy . . .

Distraught in autumn, kneeling under the chestnut trees,
seeing childhood in the conkers through my tears.
Bonkers. And me so butch in my boots down the macho
        bars . . .

Give me a break. Don't let me pine for that first love,
that faint down on the cheeks, that easy laugh
in my ears, in my lonesome heart, the day that I had to
        leave . . .

Sweet Jesus, Doc, I worry I'll miss when a long time dead
the smell the smell the smell of the baby's head,
the fresh-baked grass, dammit, the new-mown bread . . .

PLUTO

When I awoke
a brand new planet
had been given a name –

    this Home I'm in,
    it has the same soap suddenly;
    so, washing my hands,
    I'm thinking *Pluto Pluto Pluto*,
    thrilled,
    beside myself.

    And then I notice things;
    brown coins of age on my face the size of ha'pennies.
    An hourglass weeping the future into the past

– and I was a boy.

I cry out now in my bath,
shocked and bereaved again
by not quite seeing us all,
half-hearing my father's laugh –
without the help and support of the woman I love.

Tangerine soap.
To think of another world out there
in the dark,
unreachable,
of what it was like.

BEACHCOMBER

If you think till it hurts
you can almost do it without getting off that chair,
scare yourself
within an inch of the heart
at the prompt of a word.
How old are you now?
This is what happens –

the child,
and not in sepia,
lives,
you can see her;
comes up the beach,
alone;
bucket and spade.
In her bucket, a starfish, seaweed,
a dozen alarming crabs
caught with string and a mussel.
Don't move.
Trow.

Go for the sound of the sea,
don't try to describe it,
get it into your head;
and then the platinum blaze of the sun as the earth seemed
    to turn away.
Now she is kneeling.

This is about something.
Harder.
The red spade
scooping a hole in the sand.
Sea-water seeping in.

The girl suddenly holding a conch, listening, sssh.
You remember that cardigan, yes?
You remember that cardigan.

But this is as close as you get.
Nearly there.
Open your eyes.
Those older, those shaking, hands cannot touch
the child
or the spade
or the sand
or the seashell on the shore;
and what
what would you have to say,
of all people,
to her
given the chance?
Exactly.

CAUL

No, I don't remember the thing itself.
I remember the word.
Amnion, inner membrane, *caul*.
I'll never be drowned.

The past is the future waiting for dreams
and will find itself there.
I came in a cloak of cool luck
and smiled at the world.

Where the man asked the woman to tell
how it felt, how it looked,
and a sailor purchased my charm
to bear to the sea.

I imagine it now, a leathery sheath
the length of a palm
empty as mine, under the waves
or spoil on a beach.

I'm all that is left of then. It spools
itself out like a film
a talented friend can recall
using speech alone.

The light of a candle seen in a caul
eased from my crown that day,
when all but this living noun
was taken away.

AWAY AND SEE

Away and see an ocean suck at a boiled sun
and say to someone things I'd blush even to dream.
Slip off your dress in a high room over the harbour.
Write to me soon.

New fruits sing on the flipside of night in a market
of language, light, a tune from the chapel nearby
stopping you dead, the peach in your palm respiring.
Taste it for me.

Away and see the things that words give a name to, the flight
of syllables, wingspan stretching a noun. Test words
wherever they live; listen and touch, smell, believe.
Spell them with love.

Skedaddle. Somebody chaps at the door at a year's end,
    hopeful.
Away and see who it is. Let in the new, the vivid,
horror and pity, passion, the stranger holding the future.
Ask him his name.

Nothing's the same as anything else. Away and see
for yourself. Walk. Fly. Take a boat till land reappears,
altered forever, ringing its bells, alive. Go on. G'on. Gon.
Away and see.

DRUNK

Suddenly the rain is hilarious.
The moon wobbles in the dusk.

What a laugh. Unseen frogs
belch in the damp grass.

The strange perfumes of darkening trees.
Cheap red wine

and the whole world a mouth.
Give me a double, a kiss.

SMALL FEMALE SKULL

With some surprise, I balance my small female skull in my
      hands.
What is it like? An ocarina? Blow in its eye.
It cannot cry, holds my breath only as long as I exhale,
mildly alarmed now, into the hole where the nose was,
press my ear to its grin. A vanishing sigh.

For some time, I sit on the lavatory seat with my head
in my hands, appalled. It feels much lighter than I'd thought;
the weight of a deck of cards, a slim volume of verse,
but with something else, as though it could levitate.
      Disturbing.
So why do I kiss it on the brow, my warm lips to its papery
      bone,

and take it to the mirror to ask for a gottle of geer?
I rinse it under the tap, watch dust run away, like sand
from a swimming-cap, then dry it – firstborn – gently
with a towel. I see the scar where I fell for sheer love
down treacherous stairs, and read that shattering day like
      braille.

Love, I murmur to my skull, then, louder, other grand
      words,
shouting the hollow nouns in a white-tiled room.
Downstairs they will think I have lost my mind. No. I only
      weep
into these two holes here, or I'm grinning back at the joke,
      this is
a friend of mine. See, I hold her face in trembling, passionate
      hands.

MOMENTS OF GRACE

I dream through a wordless, familiar place.
The small boat of the day sails into morning,
past the postman with his modest haul, the full trees
which sound like the sea, leaving my hands free
to remember. Moments of grace. *Like this.*

Shaken by first love and kissing a wall. *Of course.*
The dried ink on the palms then ran suddenly wet,
a glistening blue name in each fist. I sit now
in a kind of sly trance, hoping I will not feel me
breathing too close across time. A face to the name. *Gone.*

The chimes of mothers calling in children
at dusk. *Yes.* It seems we live in those staggering years
only to haunt them; the vanishing scents
and colours of infinite hours like a melting balloon
in earlier hands. The boredom since.

Memory's caged bird won't fly. These days
we are adjectives, nouns. In moments of grace
we were verbs, the secret of poems, talented.
A thin skin lies on the language. We stare
deep in the eyes of strangers, look for the doing words.

Now I smell you peeling an orange in the other room.
Now I take off my watch, let a minute unravel
in my hands, listen and look as I do so,
and mild loss opens my lips like *No.*
Passing, you kiss the back of my neck. A blessing.

FIRST LOVE

Waking, with a dream of first love forming real words,
as close to my lips as lipstick, I speak your name,
after a silence of years, into the pillow, and the power
of your name brings me here to the window, naked,
to say it again to a garden shaking with light.

This was a child's love, and yet I clench my eyes
till the pictures return, unfocused at first, then
almost clear, an old film played at a slow speed.
All day I will glimpse it, in windows of changing sky,
in mirrors, my lover's eyes, wherever you are.

And later a star, long dead, here, seems precisely
the size of a tear. Tonight, a love-letter out of a dream
stammers itself in my heart. Such faithfulness.
You smile in my head on the last evening. Unseen
flowers suddenly pierce and sweeten the air.

CAFÉ ROYAL

He arrives too late to tell him how it will be.
Oscar is gone. Alone, he orders hock,
sips in the style of an earlier century
in glamorous mirrors under the clocks.

He would like to live then now, suddenly find
himself early, nod to Harris and Shaw;
then sit alone at a table, biding his time
till the Lord of Language stands at the door.

So tall. Breathing. He is the boy who fades away
as Oscar laughingly draws up a chair.
A hundred years on, he longs at the bar to say
Dear, I know where you're going. Don't go there.

But pays for his drink, still tasting the wine's sweet fruit,
and leaves. It matters how everyone dies,
he thinks, half-smiles at an older man in a suit
who stares at his terrible, wonderful eyes.

CRUSH

The older she gets,
the more she awakes
with somebody's face strewn in her head
like petals which once made a flower.

What everyone does
is sit by a desk
and stare at the view, till the time
where they live reappears. Mostly in words.

Imagine a girl
turning to see
love stand by a window, taller,
clever, anointed with sudden light.

Yes, like an angel then,
to be truthful now.
At first a secret, erotic, mute;
today a language she cannot recall.

And we're all owed joy,
sooner or later.
The trick's to remember whenever
it was, or to see it coming.

NEVER GO BACK

In the bar where the living dead drink all day
and a jukebox reminisces in a cracked voice
there is nothing to say. You talk for hours
in agreed motifs, anecdotes shuffled and dealt
from a well-thumbed pack, snapshots. The smoky mirrors
flatter; your ghost buys a round for the parched,
old faces of the past. Never return
to the space where you left time pining till it died.

Outside, the streets tear litter in their thin hands,
a tired wind whistles through the blackened stumps of houses
at a limping dog. *God, this is an awful place*
says the friend, the alcoholic, whose head is a negative
of itself. You listen and nod, bereaved. Baby,
what you owe to this place is unpayable
in the only currency you have. So drink up. Shut up,
then get them in again. Again. And never go back.

                    *   *   *

The house where you were one of the brides
has cancer. It prefers to be left alone
nursing its growth and cracks, each groan and creak
accusing as you climb the stairs to the bedroom
and draw your loved body on blurred air
with the simple power of loss. All the lies
told here, and all the cries of love,
suddenly swarm in the room, sting you, disappear.

You shouldn't be here. You follow your shadow
through the house, discover that objects held
in the hands can fill a room with pain.
You lived here only to stand here now
and half-believe that you did. A small moment
of death by a window myopic with rain.
You learn this lesson hard, speechless, slamming
the front door, shaking plaster confetti from your hair.

        *   *   *

A taxi implying a hearse takes you slowly,
the long way round, to the station. The driver
looks like death. The places you knew
have changed their names by neon, cheap tricks
in a theme-park with no theme. Sly sums of money
wink at you in the cab. At a red light,
you wipe a slick of cold sweat from the glass
for a drenched whore to stare you full in the face.

You pay to get out, pass the *Welcome To* sign
on the way to the barrier, an emigrant
for the last time. The train sighs
and pulls you away, rewinding the city like a film,
snapping it off at the river. You go for a drink,
released by a journey into nowhere, nowhen,
and all the way home you forget. Forget. Already
the fires and lights come on wherever you live.

OSLO

What you do. Follow the slow tram
into the night. Wear your coat with the hood.
You're foreign here. The town reveals itself
the way the one you live in never could.

Not to speak the language makes you
innocent again, invisible. But if you like
you bribe the bellboy in this grand hotel
to tell where the casino is, a blue light

over its door. You're in. A cool drink.
Your money changed. Too early yet,
at ten o'clock, for scented, smoking, silent
men to gather round and, you bet, bet and bet.

This life, you win some, lose some. Then?
You want to go home. With only a numbered key,
you take the shortcut past the palace, through
the tall Norwegian wood. For now, you're lucky –

across the world, someone loves you hard enough
to sieve a single star from this dark sky.

THE GRAMMAR OF LIGHT

Even barely enough light to find a mouth,
and bless both with a meaningless O, teaches,
spells out. The way a curtain opened at night
lets in neon, or moon, or a car's hasty glance,
and paints for a moment someone you love, pierces.

And so many mornings to learn; some
when the day is wrung from damp, grey skies
and rooms come on for breakfast
in the town you are leaving early. The way
a wasteground weeps glass tears at the end of a street.

Some fluent, showing you how the trees
in the square think in birds, telepathise. The way
the waiter balances light in his hands, the coins
in his pocket silver, and a young bell shines
in its white tower ready to tell.

Even a saucer of rain in a garden at evening
speaks to the eye. Like the little fires
from allotments, undressing in veils of mauve smoke
as you walk home under the muted lamps,
perplexed. The way the shy stars go stuttering on.

And at midnight, a candle next to the wine
slurs its soft wax, flatters. Shadows
circle the table. The way all faces blur
to dreams of themselves held in the eyes.
The flare of another match. The way everything dies.

VALENTINE

Not a red rose or a satin heart.

I give you an onion.
It is a moon wrapped in brown paper.
It promises light
like the careful undressing of love.

Here.
It will blind you with tears
like a lover.
It will make your reflection
a wobbling photo of grief.

I am trying to be truthful.

Not a cute card or a kissogram.

I give you an onion.
Its fierce kiss will stay on your lips,
possessive and faithful
as we are,
for as long as we are.

Take it.
Its platinum loops shrink to a wedding-ring,
if you like.
Lethal.
Its scent will cling to your fingers,
cling to your knife.

SLEEPING

Under the dark warm waters of sleep
your hands part me.
I am dreaming you anyway.

Your mouth is hot fruit, wet, strange,
night-fruit I taste with my opening mouth;
my eyes closed.

You, you. Your breath flares into fervent words
which explode in my head. Then you ask, push,
for an answer.

And this is how we sleep. You're in now, hard,
demanding; so I dream more fiercely, dream
till it hurts

that this is for real, yes, I feel it.
When you hear me, you hold on tight, frantic,
as if we were drowning.

STEAM

Not long ago so far, a lover and I
in a room of steam –

a sly, thirsty, silvery word – lay down,
opposite ends, and vanished.

Quite recently, if one of us sat up,
or stood, or stretched, naked,

a nude pose in soft pencil
behind tissue paper

appeared, rubbed itself out, slow,
with a smoky cloth.

Say a matter of months. This hand reaching
through the steam

to touch the real thing, shockingly there,
not a ghost at all.

CLOSE

Lock the door. In the dark journey of our night,
two childhoods stand in the corner of the bedroom
watching the way we take each other to bits
to stare at our heart. I hear a story
told in sleep in a lost accent. You know the words.

Undress. A suitcase crammed with secrets
bursts in the wardrobe at the foot of the bed.
Dress again. Undress. You have me like a drawing,
erased, coloured in, untitled, signed by your tongue.
The name of a country written in red on my palm,

unreadable. I tell myself where I live now,
but you move in close till I shake, homeless,
further than that. A coin falls from the bedside table,
spinning its heads and tails. How the hell
can I win. How can I lose. Tell me again.

Love won't give in. It makes a hired room tremble
with the pity of bells, a cigarette smoke itself
next to a full glass of wine, time ache
into space, space, wants no more talk. Now
it has me where I want me, now you, you do.

Put out the light. Years stand outside on the street
looking up to an open window, black as our mouth
which utters its tuneless song. The ghosts of ourselves,
behind and before us, throng in a mirror, blind,
laughing and weeping. They know who we are.

ADULTERY

Wear dark glasses in the rain.
Regard what was unhurt
as though through a bruise.
Guilt. A sick, green tint.

New gloves, money tucked in the palms,
the handshake crackles. Hands
can do many things. Phone.
Open the wine. Wash themselves. Now

you are naked under your clothes all day,
slim with deceit. Only the once
brings you alone to your knees,
miming, more, more, older and sadder,

creative. Suck a lie with a hole in it
on the way home from a lethal, thrilling night
up against a wall, faster. Language
unpeels to a lost cry. You're a bastard.

Do it do it do it. Sweet darkness
in the afternoon; a voice in your ear
telling you how you are wanted,
which way, now. A telltale clock

wiping the hours from its face, your face
on a white sheet, gasping, radiant, yes.
Pay for it in cash, fiction, cab-fares back
to the life which crumbles like a wedding-cake.

Paranoia for lunch; too much
to drink, as a hand on your thigh
tilts the restaurant. You know all about love,
don't you. Turn on your beautiful eyes

for a stranger who's dynamite in bed, again
and again; a slow replay in the kitchen
where the slicing of innocent onions
scalds you to tears. Then, selfish autobiographical sleep

in a marital bed, the tarnished spoon of your body
stirring betrayal, your heart over-ripe at the core.
You're an expert, darling; your flowers
dumb and explicit on nobody's birthday.

So write the script – illness and debt,
a ring thrown away in a garden
no moon can heal, your own words
commuting to bile in your mouth, terror –

and all for the same thing twice. And all
for the same thing twice. You did it.
What. Didn't you. Fuck. Fuck. No. That was
the wrong verb. This is only an abstract noun.

HAVISHAM

Beloved sweetheart bastard. Not a day since then
I haven't wished him dead. Prayed for it
so hard I've dark green pebbles for eyes,
ropes on the back of my hands I could strangle with.

Spinster. I stink and remember. Whole days
in bed cawing Nooooo at the wall; the dress
yellowing, trembling if I open the wardrobe;
the slewed mirror, full-length, her, myself, who did this

to me? Puce curses that are sounds not words.
Some nights better, the lost body over me,
my fluent tongue in its mouth in its ear
then down till I suddenly bite awake. Love's

hate behind a white veil; a red balloon bursting
in my face. Bang. I stabbed at a wedding-cake.
Give me a male corpse for a long slow honeymoon.
Don't think it's only the heart that b-b-b-breaks.

THE SUICIDE

Small dark hours with a bitter moon buffed by the smudgy
    clouds
till it gleams with resentment.
I dress in a shroud. Despair
laced with a little glee.
Leave it to me.

Never never never
never enough.
The horrid smiling mouths
pout on the wallpaper. Kisses
on a collar. Lies. Blood.
My body is a blank page I will write on.

Famous.

Nobody drinks with their whole face.
I do.
Nobody's ears are confessionals.
Mine are.
Eyes in the glass like squids. Sexy.

I get out the knives. Who wants
a bloody valentine pumping its love hate love?
Utterly selfless
I lie back under the lightbulb.
Something like a cat claws from my head, spiteful.

Fuck off.
Worship.

This will kill my folks.

STUFFED

I put two yellow peepers in an owl.
Wow. I fix the grin of Crocodile.
Spiv. I sew the slither of an eel.

I jerk, kick-start, the back hooves of a mule.
Wild. I hold a red rag to a bull.
Mad. I spread the feathers of a gull.

I screw a tight snarl to a weasel.
Fierce. I stitch the flippers on a seal.
Splayed. I pierce the heartbeat of a quail.

I like her to be naked and to kneel.
Tame. My motionless, my living doll.
Mute. And afterwards I like her not to tell.

FRAUD

Firstly, I changed my name
to that of a youth I knew for sure had bought it in 1940,
    Rotterdam.
Private M.
I was my own poem,
pseudonym,
rule of thumb.
What was my aim?
To change from a bum
to a billionaire. I spoke the English. Mine was a scam
involving pensions, papers, politicians in-and-out of their
    pram.
And I was to blame.

For what? There's a gnome
in Zürich knows more than people assume.
There's a military man, Jerusalem
way, keeping schtum.
Then there's Him –
for whom
I paid for a butch and femme
to make him come.
And all of the crème
de la crème
considered me scum.

Poverty's dumb.
Take it from me, Sonny Jim,
learn to lie in the mother-tongue of the motherfucker you
    want to charm.
They're all the same,
turning their wide blind eyes to crime.
And who gives a damn

when the keys to a second home
are pressed in his palm,
or polaroids of a Night of Shame
with a Boy on the Game
are passed his way at the A.G.M.?

So read my lips. Mo-ney. Pow-er. Fame.
And had I been asked, in my time,
in my puce and prosperous prime,
if I recalled the crumbling slum
of my Daddy's home,
if I was a shit, a sham,
if I'd done immeasurable harm,
I could have replied with a dream:
the water that night was calm
and with my enormous mouth, in bubbles and blood
    and phlegm,
I gargled my name.

THE BIOGRAPHER

Because you are dead,
I stand at your desk,
my fingers caressing the grooves in the wood
your initials made;
and I manage a quote,
echo one of your lines in the small, blue room
where an early daguerreotype shows you
excitedly staring out
from behind your face,
the thing that made you yourself
still visibly there,
like a hood and a cloak of light.
The first four words that I write are your name.

I'm a passionate man
with a big advance
who's loved your work since he was a boy;
but the night
I slept alone in your bed,
the end of a fire going out in the grate,
I came awake –
certain, had we ever met,
you wouldn't have wanted me,
or needed me,
would barely have noticed me at all.
Guilt and rage
hardened me then,
and later I felt your dislike
chilling the air
as I drifted away.
Your wallpaper green and crimson and gold.

How close can I get
to the sound of your voice
which Emma Elizabeth Hibbert described –
lively, eager and lightly-pitched,
with none of the later, bitter edge.
Cockney, a little.
In London Town,
the faces you wrote
leer and gape and plead at my feet.
Once, high on Hungerford Bridge,
a stew and tangle of rags, sniffed by a dog, stood, spoke,
spat at the shadow I cast,
at the meagre shadow I cast in my time.
I heard the faraway bells of St Paul's as I ran.

Maestro. Monster. Mummy's Boy.
My Main Man.
I write you and write you for five hard years.
I have an affair with a thespian girl –
you would have approved –
then I snivel home to my wife.
Her poems and jam.
Her forgiveness.
Her violent love.
And this is a life.
I print it out.
I print it out.
In all of your mirrors, my face;
with its smallish, its quizzical eyes,
its cheekbones, its sexy jaw,
its talentless, dustjacket smile.

THE WINDOWS

How do you earn a life going on
behind yellow windows, writing at night
the Latin names of plants for a garden,
opening the front door to a wet dog?

Those you love forgive you, clearly,
with steaming casseroles and red wine.
It's the same film down all the suburban streets,
It's A Wonderful Life. How do you learn it?

What you hear – the doorbell's familiar chime.
What you touch – the clean, warm towels.
What you see what you smell what you taste
all tangible to the stranger passing your gate.

There you are again, in a room where those early hyacinths
surely sweeten the air, and the right words wait
in the dictionaries, on the tip of the tongue you touch
in a kiss, drawing your crimson curtains now

against dark hours. And again, in a kitchen,
the window ajar, sometimes the sound of your radio
or the scent of your food, and a cat in your arms,
a child in your arms, a lover. Such vivid flowers.

DISGRACE

But one day we woke to disgrace; our house
a coldness of rooms, each nursing
a thickening cyst of dust and gloom.
We had not been home in our hearts for months.

And how our words changed. Dead flies in a web.
How they stiffened and blackened. Cherished italics
suddenly sour on our tongues, obscenities
spraying themselves on the wall in my head.

Woke to your clothes like a corpse on the floor,
the small deaths of lightbulbs pining all day
in my ears, their echoes audible tears;
nothing we would not do to make it worse

and worse. Into the night with the wrong language,
waving and pointing, the shadows of hands
huge in the bedroom. Dreamed of a naked crawl
from a dead place over the other; both of us. Woke.

Woke to the absence of grace; the still-life
of a meal, untouched, wine-bottle, empty, ashtray,
full. In our sullen kitchen, the fridge
hardened its cool heart, selfish as art, hummed.

To a bowl of apples rotten to the core. Lame shoes
empty in the hall where our voices asked
for a message after the tone, the telephone
pressing its ear to distant, invisible lips.

And our garden bowing its head, vulnerable flowers
unseen in the dusk as we shouted in silhouette.
Woke to the screaming alarm, the banging door,
the house-plants trembling in their brittle soil. Total

disgrace. Up in the dark to stand at the window,
counting the years to arrive there, faithless,
unpenitent. Woke to the meaningless stars, you
and me both, lost. Inconsolable vowels from the next room.

ROOM

One chair to sit in,
a greasy dusk wrong side of the tracks,
and watch the lodgers' lights come on in the other rooms.

No curtains yet. A cool lightbulb
waiting for a moth. Hard silence.
The roofs of terraced houses stretch from here to how many
     months.

Room. One second-hand bed
to remind of a death, somewhen. Room.
Then clouds the colour of smokers' lungs. Then what.

In a cold black window, a face
takes off its glasses and stares out again.
Night now; the giftless moon and a cat pissing on a wall. £90pw.

MEAN TIME

The clocks slid back an hour
and stole light from my life
as I walked through the wrong part of town,
mourning our love.

And, of course, unmendable rain
fell to the bleak streets
where I felt my heart gnaw
at all our mistakes.

If the darkening sky could lift
more than one hour from this day
there are words I would never have said
nor have heard you say.

But we will be dead, as we know,
beyond all light.
These are the shortened days
and the endless nights.

PRAYER

Some days, although we cannot pray, a prayer
utters itself. So, a woman will lift
her head from the sieve of her hands and stare
at the minims sung by a tree, a sudden gift.

Some nights, although we are faithless, the truth
enters our hearts, that small familiar pain;
then a man will stand stock-still, hearing his youth
in the distant Latin chanting of a train.

Pray for us now. Grade I piano scales
console the lodger looking out across
a Midlands town. Then dusk, and someone calls
a child's name as though they named their loss.

Darkness outside. Inside, the radio's prayer –
Rockall. Malin. Dogger. Finisterre.

Some recent and forthcoming poetry from Anvil

BEI DAO
Old Snow
Translated by Bonnie McDougall & Chen Maiping

NORMAN CAMERON
Collected Poems
AND SELECTED TRANSLATIONS
Edited by Warren Hope & Jonathan Barker

CAROL ANN DUFFY
William and the Ex-Prime Minister

HARRY GUEST
Coming to Terms

MICHAEL HAMBURGER
Roots in the Air

JAMES HARPUR
A Vision of Comets

MARIUS KOCIEJOWSKI
Doctor Honoris Causa

CHARLES MADGE
Of Love, Time and Places
SELECTED POEMS

PABLO NERUDA
The Captain's Verses
Translated by Brian Cole

DENNIS O'DRISCOLL
Long Story Short

PHILIP SHERRARD
In the Sign of the Rainbow
SELECTED POEMS 1940–1989

SUE STEWART
Inventing the Fishes

A catalogue of our publications is available on request

Other books by Carol Ann Duffy

STANDING FEMALE NUDE

'... a book that marks the debut of a genuine and original poet.'
— ROBERT NYE in *The Times*

'Carol Ann Duffy is a very pure poet... It is good to see a crusading sensibility refusing to surrender any touch of art to the urgency of its cause.'
— PETER PORTER in *The Observer*

SELLING MANHATTAN

'... not only a fresh voice but a dexterity with language, that glorious juggling which poets sometimes achieve with a sense of surprise even to themselves.... Her range of subject and theme is unusually wide and she writes with an authority which, at her best, conceals the merely personal.'
— ELIZABETH JENNINGS in *The Independent*

'*Selling Manhattan* is one of those rare books that is immediately enjoyable yet will repay many re-readings. Buy it.'
— VERNON SCANNELL in *Poetry Review*

THE OTHER COUNTRY

'*The Other Country* is a slim volume like few that have been published recently: urgent, packed with future classics – a book that proclaims that poetry is alive. Be in there early.'
— PETER FORBES in *The Guardian*

'Her perfect pitch and subtle sense of rhythm tap the roots of memory and consciousness to profound effect.'
— DENNIS O'DRISCOLL in *Poetry Review*

'It voices political-erotic challenge, always knows where it's going, and has serious fun on the way.... Duffy's is a cabaret art, and her leg-flinging technique (the one-word sentences and buried rhymes, the dizzying control of line) can say practically anything.'
— RUTH PADEL in the *TLS*